To Shine a Light

For Susana,

Thank you for your love, prayers and belief that this book should be written to bring healing and hope to many because of life & light in Jesus Christ.

May God's favor be upon this with wisdom and insight to set the captives free.

Happy Easter, J.

To Shine a Light:
A GUIDE TO RECOVERY FROM SATANIC RITUAL ABUSE

Including the author's personal journey

Suzanne Violetta

Copyright ©2015 Suzanne Violetta
All rights reserved. No part of this publication may be used or reproduced, stored or entered into a retrieval system, transmitted, photocopied, recorded, or otherwise reproduced in any form by any mechanical or electronic means, without the prior written permission of the author, except for brief quotations used in articles and reviews.
First Edition: March 2015

Editor: Marianne Harkin
Cover Art: Pamela Violetta

ISBN 10: 1505954940
ISBN 13: 9781505954944
Library of Congress Control Number: 2015900571
CreateSpace Independent Publishing Platform
North Charleston, South Carolina

ENDORSEMENTS

[The author has] done an excellent job on a subject that will "open the eyes" of many people, including many Christians and Pastors who haven't really believed in such evil. I applaud you in this work.

Pastor James Isom
Youth with a Mission ministry
Founder, Ephesians 5:18 Life Ministries

Throughout the world, including our own community, people talk about practices that range from séances to sacrifices. Most people don't know the scope and enormity of these satanic activities, except the participants and victims. Within the satanic circle, secrets and shame abound. When victims finally share their experiences, they are not believed, even in the safety of therapy sessions.

Suzanne Violetta bravely shares the trauma that she and her sister suffered as little girls, and came to understand in their adult lives. Their compelling stories, therapeutic journeys, and healing processes give hope to others who are victims of Satanic Ritual Abuse.

A chapter on successful treatments encourages victims and therapists to work together to help victims of these atrocities on their journey from despair to hope and health.

Patricia Doane
LCPC, LCADC, CSAT, CMAT

Many therapists have no experience with what has been labeled "Satanic Ritual Abuse." This book can greatly aid their understanding and provide guidance for their therapeutic work with clients.

Clients who have encountered this type of abuse can benefit from discussing topics in this book in sessions with their therapist rather than reading the book on their own. In presenting the material in this way, the client can receive appropriate and safe information without being overwhelmed.

SRA Survivor
MS, MA, LPC, RN, CS-P

It takes courage to confront a topic such as Satanic Ritual Abuse (SRA). For those who are starting to look for answers about SRA, this book provides the perspective and resources of both a survivor and a therapist.

- Suzanne O'Connor, Psy.D.

To Katy.

For teaching me how to receive
and give unconditional love.

*"For you shall know the truth,
And the truth shall set you free."*

Table of Contents

Acknowledgements xi
A Note from the Author xiii
Preface xv
Introduction xix

Chapter 1   What is SRA? 1
Chapter 2   A Brief History of SRA 5
             Personal Perspective 8
Chapter 3   The Signs and Symptoms of Satanic Ritual Abuse ... 11
Chapter 4   Client Perspective 15
             Personal Perspective 18
Chapter 5   Illness Associated with SRA 23
             Personal Perspective 26
Chapter 6   Dissociation and Other Disorders 29
Chapter 7   Attachment 35
Chapter 8   Exploring the Past 37
             Personal Perspective 42
Chapter 9   Treatment for Ritual Abuse Survivors 43
             Personal Reflection 52
Chapter 10   Hope for the Future 55
Chapter 11   Conclusion 59

Appendix	Satanic Calendar	62
	Satanic Symbols	63
	Recommended Reading	67
	References	73

Acknowledgements

For the many women in the support groups, prayer groups, and professional organizations that were a source of encouragement, inspiration, and belief that this book should be written,
Thank you for your under girding prayers.

For the professors, therapists, and colleagues who could envision this book long before I had the courage to start writing,
Thank you for your validation.

For the mentors that infused me with faith, hope, and trust that this was a worthy endeavor,
Your love and wisdom took my breath away.

For the wordsmith, witness, persistence-in-Chief, encourager and editor who took painful pages written with tear-stained marks and produced a book,
Thank you for your translation from terror to testimony.

For my husband, I thank you for the years of compassion, even when we did not know the cause of the pain. I love you.

A Note from the Author

THIS BOOK HAS NOT BEEN an easy one to write. There have been countless times in this journey when I wanted nothing more than to shred the pages I had written and put a match to them. To write of these memories is, in many cases, to relive them, and for me that can be dangerous territory. But I made a promise.

As my sister, Katy*, lay dying, she asked me to shine a light on this harrowing abuse, to let the world know that not only does satanic ritual abuse exist, but is more widespread than one could imagine. Katy wanted me to tell our story, to spread the word in the widest way possible so that others could get the help they so desperately need when they have been exposed to this abuse.

Many males are victims of SRA, too. The preponderance of victims are female. Since this book is about my sister's and my experiences, I will write from the perspective of a female child.

I promised Katy that I would write the book and this is the fulfillment of that promise. There is hope and there can be healing. Satanic ritual abuse might change your life, but it does not have to define you. My goal with these pages is to guide you toward the light of that healing.

- Suzanne Violetta

Although this is a true story, names and places have been changed to protect the identities of those involved.

Preface

WHERE TO BEGIN? THIS PROJECT has been many, many years in the making for a myriad of reasons. The first of these is that my suppressed memories have been surfacing for many years, and continue to do so.

Initially, the memories were like a flashbulb from a camera. They came "out of nowhere." They were not connecting to anything I was thinking about or doing during the day. Fast, very quickly; here then gone. I thought "how weird was that?" Those types of memories happened spontaneously for about a year. Do you remember where you were on 9/11? We all do. This is an example of an intrinsic memory. It is encoded with emotional content of the event. More about this in a later chapter.

Then slowly, more and more memories came. They were now very vivid with colors, shapes, sounds, and again, I thought "these are really bizarre." Around the same timeframe, I was having nightmares where I would wake up terrified or crying and shaking. Then came panic attacks almost daily, then intense anxiety and cascading depression.

At this point, I was barely functioning. I went to my medical doctor, a very compassionate internist, who diagnosed me with clinical depression and anxiety. She prescribed 10 mg of Paxil and 25 mg of Trazodone.

I began to feel better physically, but still had the memories. I had pulled my back out and went to a chiropractor. You will read more about that in a later chapter.

Gradually I started to come out of the deep despair. It took medication, therapy, supportive friends, family, and prayers. Today, many years later, I tell my story to bring hope and healing to victims who become survivors.

Another reason for my writing this book has to do with the wishes of family members not to be included. I want to tell their stories but they, whether because of insistence that they did not experience the same things I did or denial that it happened to them, do not want them told. So I honor that. In my therapy practice with SRA survivors and in talking with many colleagues who are survivors, it is not uncommon for one or two children out of a family with more children to be the ones chosen for victimization and indoctrination. It seems as if the oldest and middle children are the ones targeted.

I have spoken to my other siblings at great length and in great detail, and I am convinced that they did not suffer the horrors that my sister and I underwent. The reason for this may never be known to me, but I am grateful that they did not suffer as my sister and I did.

As I grew up, I remember being very protective of my sisters and brother. When they were punished I felt as if I had not done my part as their big sister. I certainly developed a co-dependent nature but it seemed to go much deeper than that. Was there survivor guilt of living among the horror? Were there children before me that were sacrificed? Most of my life, I lived with tremendous shame around issues that should not have been shameful.

My indecision on how to tell my story was another factor. There is not, to my knowledge, a clinician who has written a portrayal of this process and used these experiences with faux clients to educate, assess, and explore the long-term ramifications of this type of abuse. Another possibility that held great interest for me was to create a guide for survivors to help them deal with their trauma. To give hope to victims through appropriate trauma treatment, medication, support networks, and prayer is to give them hope for not only survival, but the prospect of living a full and productive life.

A possible reason for this lack of published information might be the controversy over "false memory syndrome" that surfaced in the 1980's when a tremendous outpouring of claims over satanic ritual abuse surfaced. The general feeling of the psychological community at the time was that the memories were false ones brought on by coaching by overzealous or less than scrupulous therapists. Now, 30 years later, evidence to support the truth behind the memories has emerged.

In the end, I decided that the best course would be to combine these aspects. This is my story and it will be told in a way, not only to pay homage to my sister and other victims of satanic ritual abuse, but also to help myself and others, therapists and survivors alike.

My journey to survival and recovery from satanic ritual abuse was, and is, at times harrowing, but it must be told. My goal is to help others who have known the terror of growing up in such an environment, and I can only do that by telling the truth.

The contents of these pages are difficult in context. I advise that the reading be done with a therapeutic/faith-based support system if you are a survivor. For therapists, please know that there may be educational components that will be helpful as your new skill sets; proceed with caution.

Introduction

My memories began to resurface at age 44. I was sitting in my chiropractor's office, getting ready for an adjustment of my neck and shoulders. As the doctor began to work on me, I screamed and burst into tears. The doctor, shocked, asked "What did I do? Did I hurt you?" When I was able to catch my breath, I answered, "No, I had a flashback of being hung by a rope in the basement." Thus began the return of my forgotten childhood. The chiropractor, a kind man who listened to my story in the ensuing months, told me, "You really ought to tell your story." And so I shall. As is so often stated in the psychotherapeutic community, the body remembers.

I was born in Arkansas in 1943, the first of four children to my mother, a professional singer and my father, a medical intern. By the time I was two years old, my dad was a lieutenant colonel in the Air Force, and we were moved to a base in South Dakota, where he was assigned to obstetrics/gynecology at the base hospital. Shortly after we arrived, my sister Katy was born. Mother was busy being an officer's wife with all its attendant duties, so a nanny was hired to care for the children. The nanny lived with us for over two years until, when my second sister was six months old, my mother abruptly fired her for her odd behavior and questionable child-rearing methods. At five years old, it wasn't a decision I questioned, but resurfaced memories assure me that the nanny was deeply involved in the abuse.

My sisters and brother and I were then raised by a distracted mother and a busy father. I was seven, and my sisters were five and three years old, and my brother was a newborn baby. We grew up and went to high school, just like our friends. We had picnics, we rode horses, we went to prom. We did the things that normal people do.

My mother was beautiful, warm, engaging with everyone but her own children. Her mission in life, for reasons unknown to me at the time, was to keep busy. She was never angry, always soft-spoken, never a gossip but somehow distracted by something unseen. My mother met my father when she was 14 years old. She and he were a couple for the next 11 years – through high school, college, and his medical school education, internship, and residency. They married when she was 27 years old. Throughout their courtship, my mother was successful in her own right – as a singer and later as the host of her own radio show. Once they were married, though, my mother gave up her career to become a wife and mother.

Dad was your typical larger-than-life presence – handsome, charismatic, engaging, and willing to dip into "bad boy" habits – drugs, alcohol, gambling, and women – the life of the party. Everyone loved him. He pursued his practice in obstetrics and pediatrics on the Air Force base where we lived, delivering and caring for the children of the town. My father was often called away in the evening and stayed away all night long – supposedly to deliver a baby, which may or may not always have been the truth.

By all accounts, I had a normal childhood. I remember Easter baskets and ice skating; piano lessons and cheerleading and ROTC. Up until I was 44, I thought I had a great, or at least normal childhood. More accurately put, I never thought about it at all. If there was a blank spot in my memory, I did nothing to address it or try to recapture the information. I remained unaware of how I really grew up until that day in the chiropractor's office when my world tilted on its axis.

The memories have shown me the truth of my life. They remind me that my mother wasn't only busy, but almost robotically so at times.

At other times she seemed drugged and unaware of what was going on around her. The memories also serve to remind me that my father was a controlling addict who had oral sex with me in a closet when I was around five years old. My youngest sister remembers our basement as nothing more than a spooky place with a lot of bad smells coming from the toilet. I remember the same toilet, complete with the bodies of disemboweled chickens, ducks and rabbits that were sacrificed on the makeshift altar near it. It is so disorienting to have a normal life with back and forth, day-to-day activities where there are the extremes and horrific exposure, which is completely abnormal. It is difficult to believe in yourself.

My memories have also made sense of the illnesses I have suffered – depression, anxiety, Post-Traumatic Stress Disorder (PTSD). To survive SRA means to have developed any number of illnesses, attachment disorder, suicide ideation, and Dissociative Identity Disorder (DID) among them, as well as the ones mentioned in a later chapter. Getting to the root of my issues, just knowing that there is a valid reason for them, is, in a way, a relief. Knowing, as they say, is half the battle.

Once I knew my core issues, I was able to overcome them through the help of family, faith, and therapy. Now I am able to tell my story from a unique perspective: that of SRA survivor, therapist, and woman of unwavering faith in the Triune God.

Repressed memories have long been the subject of controversy. How can they be trusted when a less than scrupulous clinician may have actually implanted the memories? But that is not what happened with me, or with my sister. Our memories reanimated spontaneously many years later, without help from anyone. The memories became intrinsic (memory-based) rather than extrinsic (externally-based). What we remember, and how it has affected our lives, needs to be told, must be explored, and cannot be dismissed as "false memories." When you don't believe yourself and others do not believe you, the truth will set you free. We lived through these horrors, we survived, and we thrived. It is time now to help others through the same experience.

A thorough examination of the practice of Satanic Ritual Abuse will be provided in this book, as well as the signs and symptoms of such abuse and the kind of therapy it takes to make a survivor whole again. My sister and I survived. It is my fervent hope that you will, too.

CHAPTER 1

What is SRA?

Why are you cast down, O my soul?
And why are you disquieted within me?
Hope in God, for I shall yet praise Him
For the help of His countenance

- PSALM 42:5

SATANIC RITUAL ABUSE, ALSO KNOWN as sadistic ritual abuse, has been defined as:
A secret, organized process containing Satanic symbols, rituals, chants; bizarre and unbelievable tortures, and sacrifices that are performed systematically to install fear into the victim, to indoctrinate and program him/her to come under the control of Satanists (North American Association of Christians in Social Work - NACSW, 2011).

In my personal experience, SRA was:

- Years of numbness, avoidance, detachment
- Years of paralyzing fear
- Disorientation, poor focus, poor scholastic ability
- Dysthymia (clinical depression) and hypervigilance
- Poor relationship skills
- Confusion, mistrust, self-doubt

- Low self-esteem
- Poor boundaries

The cult members target their own children and animals for torture and sacrifice. They hide behind the curtain of social groups or clubs. Their "cover story" is that they are merely friends who get together on a regular basis. But a closer look reveals that the times they meet usually dovetails with the satanic calendar. They appear normal, but they are not normal at all. (See Appendix).

The children are the key: the earlier they are indoctrinated into the ways of SRA, the better for the cult members, because infants have not yet begun to develop ego and are better manipulated. When they are subjected to SRA, they don't fight back. Children who are programmed from birth cannot resist the abuse in any way because they have never known anything approaching normalcy in their lives.

The Extreme Abuse Survey (Becker, Karriker, Overkamp & Rutz) performed in Germany in 2007 showed that of the 986 participants, an overwhelming 55% were subjected to ritualistic abuse. The participants revealed such methods of abuse as being hung upside down until passing out, being tied down to the floor inside a pentagram and tortured with various insects, snakes, and rodents, being raped and gang-raped, being impregnated and then having the fetus taken by caesarian section for the purpose of sacrifice, being told they had killed a sibling or pet, being buried alive.

Little is known about SRA groups because they shroud themselves in secrecy. While thousands of victims have come forward with their stories, to this writer's knowledge, no perpetrator ever has. The secrets must be kept. Secrets are the binds to the perpetrator. They become another layer that terrifies and holds captive. Usually it is a close family member who uses "the secret" with confounding results for years; a word, a look, a telephone call in the night with no one on the line.

Whether or not they are formally linked to the religion known as Satanism is unclear, but it is likely that these fringe groups are actually cults that are independent of any organized religion. Historical documents show the use of altars, animal and human infant sacrifice, orgies, chanting, circles and pentagrams, and the debasement of the Catholic mass. These signs and symbols are an integral part of the practice of SRA.

Satanic ritual abuse is generational. Where or why it actually begins is not known, but once established, the practice is often passed from parent to child, generation after generation. In my own case, I believe the practice started with my paternal grandfather or even his mother. So the victim continues to become the perpetrator until the cycle is broken, usually because the child flees the parents' influence and control as soon as he or she is able. In my experience, this cycle stopped with me and my sister. This may be because the later generations are not as isolated as their predecessors; they live among ordinary people through school and social functions and provide sufficient opportunity to experience some semblance of normalcy, causing just enough doubt concerning the normalcy of their home life to permit them to choose to escape.

Are we becoming a society that can become more aware? "See something, say something" to the appropriate authorities. It is vital that the clinician and/or a client that is reading this book is able to break the cycle. There is great hope.

CHAPTER 2
A Brief History of SRA

He has shown you, O Man, what is good;
And what does the LORD require of you
But to do justly, To love mercy,
And to walk humbly with your God?

- MICAH 6:8

THE HISTORY OF SATANIC RITUAL abuse is as old as the concept of Dualism – the theory that opposing forces of good and evil do co-exist. The idea that this dichotomy can occur in one world took hold with the coming of Christianity. Unlike Judaism, which does not hold the belief that there is such a thing as Satan or Hell, Christianity acknowledges the existence of Satan. Indeed, the Catholic Church was built on the concept that evil does exist and that the only way to conquer it is through the belief in the Triune God.

The Christian faith abounds with stories of devils, particularly that of Lucifer, once an angel of God who fell from grace and was cast out of heaven and condemned to hell, thereby creating the culture of evil known as Satan's followers.

Satanic rituals appear to have taken root during the Middle Ages, when the rampant corruption pervading the Catholic Church caused many to question its stated supremacy over evil. While the Church prevailed with all its attendant wealth and privilege, the rest of the populace was suffering through the Black Death. Is it any wonder that some turned to the practice of evil, believing that there would be no solution to their problems by following the practices of a corrupt church?

When in the sixteenth century the Church was fractured from within by Martin Luther and the Reformation, the concept of Satan became more than a ritualistic hypothesis. One of the first Protestant sects, Calvinism, might have actually – although not willingly – endorsed the idea of Satanism through its belief that there are two types of people in the world: those who will attain Heaven and the rest, who are to be consigned to Hell. The practice of witchcraft and black magic became more popular and cult activity flourished. Cults and covens gave an outlet to those who believed that, either because of predestination or their sinful habits, they were unquestionably damned. If one is going to Hell, why not celebrate it by building a theology around it?

In *Out of Darkness,* David Sakheim (1992) states, "It appears to be a product of our hitherto unyielding norms and caste system that consigned to lower class people and those guilty (or allegedly guilty) of sexual indiscretions to the ranks of the damned." In other words, the strict moral codes of the Christian faith gave the weak and the poor little alternative but to turn to satanic practices. While there may be some truth to this theory, it does not explain the horrific abuse that did and does continue to pervade this little-known segment of our society.

We live in a culture of disbelief, perhaps it is beyond human nature to comprehend that which we cannot absorb as 'normal' behavior. But the facts speak for themselves. Consider the following:

- Several students of the 2014 Harvard graduating class planned a Satanic Black Mass for their graduation on-campus. When officials would not allow it, the mass was moved off campus.
- In 2014, Craigslist killer Miranda LaFerrara claimed to have ritualistically killed over 20 people. She has been involved in a satanic cult since she was 13 years old.
- In 2014, a 17-year old Houston boy murdered a 15-year old girl so that his friend, 16, could "sell his soul" to the devil.

- In 1995, a 15-year old California girl was "sacrificed to Satan" by 3 teen boys.
- The 1996 murder of Jon Benet Ramsey had distinct satanic cult overtones, although the evidence was not pursued by prosecutors in the case.
- Although the famous 1986 McMartin daycare case has been decried as a hoax, there is ample evidence that what the children claimed – ritualistic abuse, was the truth.
- In 1989 The Ritual Abuse Task Force of Los Angeles County was created specifically to identify potential sources of ritual abuse.

What are external influences that would cause this trend? Could it be that generations are growing up unchurched, and it fills a void?

Ritual sexual abuse persists today even though little is known about SRA groups because they shroud themselves in secrecy. Satanic ritual abuse predates the formal religion Satanism. It has been in practice literally for centuries. History documents the use of altars, human and animal sacrifice, chanting, orgies and the debasement of the Catholic mass as early as the fifth century. The various attitudes of society throughout the ages notwithstanding, satanic ritual abuse persists.

Personal Perspective

I come from a place of diverse perspective: as SRA survivor, therapist and a woman of unwavering faith in the Triune God. My story is one of terror, confusion, and unreality. Yet it happened. What happened to me and my sister is not the product of false memory, nor is it fantasy or fabrication. The memories that surfaced more than three decades after the fact threatened my health and wellbeing, my sanity, my very life. But through the guidance of my therapists, the belief of my family, and the steadfastness of my faith, I have emerged, not only whole, but able to help others through the memories of a life shattered by satanic ritual abuse. My sister, a beautiful, courageous woman who was made luminous through her abiding faith in the essential goodness of humanity, became a minister and spent her life in the service of God.

As our memories emerged – quite separately but at the same time – we pieced together the atrocities that had been visited upon us and tried to make sense of our past. Imagine you are four years old and you are exposed to babies being dissected on basement altars and your tiny hand is wrapped around a large kitchen knife and you are made to plunge it into a 'baby' and warned that if you ever tell, the same thing will happen to your baby sister or your pet rabbit. You will believe your perpetrators. You are now complicit in all their crimes, or so you believe. This is how brainwashing is accomplished. What is clear to me now is that, yes, we are victims, but we are also survivors. As children we belonged to the cult, and we belonged to no one. We were awash in a sea of unreality, but it was all too real for us.

Our family may have damaged our bodies and our psyches, but not our souls. My sister's spirit – her soul – remained intact until the day she died. Mine does to this day.

Dr. Bessel Van der Kolk, a noted psychologist in the field of post-traumatic stress disorder, has stated that 'the body remembers.' I believe that is why my memories found their way to my consciousness: because my body remembered, even if I didn't. I was a victim of satanic ritual abuse from the age of approximately two and a half years old until I left for college.

Therapist Perspective

The body is affected at the molecular cell level. Muscle and bone structure and each one of our organs is affected. The physical body was never intended in the 21st Century to need a fight or flight response. With the chronic exposure as an infant or toddler to horrific, life-threatening events with family members, the adrenaline courses between lifelong "fixtures" in the body. For survivors, the physical consequences are extreme: exposure to this type of complicated and extreme PTSD can also lead to heart disease, cancer, and immunological disease, gastrointestinal, esophageal, dermatological and gynecological problems. In the mental health area, depression, dysthymia and cyclothymia, bi-polar, schizophrenia, and dissociative identity disorder may be present. Addictions are rampant, trying to quiet and calm an unnamable illness that is present but unaccounted for. In the spiritual realm, belief can range from non-existent to an obsessive religious form that lacks faith or substance. When atrocities are performed in front of toddlers and children, their brains are beginning to develop their own mega rhythm. The horrific becomes the norm. As more ritual ceremonies are performed, the child's ego formation, moral conscience, and ability to know right from wrong are greatly eroded.

As can be clearly seen, the body, soul, and spirit are bound and controlled by persons knowingly using witchcraft and satanic rituals to utterly destroy the individuality of a person. Ego states are fractured in the process, and the victim is left in pieces, literally and figuratively.

CHAPTER 3

The Signs and Symptoms of Satanic Ritual Abuse

When you pass through the waters. I will be with you;
And through the rivers, they shall not overflow you.
When you walk through the fire, you shall not be burned.
Nor shall the flame scorch you.
For I am the LORD your God,
The Holy One of Israel, your Savior.

- Isaiah 43: 2, 3a

THERE ARE MANY FACETS TO successfully treating a victim of satanic ritual abuse. The first and, perhaps, most important of these is a firm belief that satanic ritual abuse really does exist. Without that certainty, a therapist cannot be of value to a victim of such abuse because above all things, an SRA survivor must have the unconditional support of a professional who will believe the horrendous stories that must be told. Victims above all else need to have their reality validated, to be told they are not crazy or imagining things.

The second requirement is a comprehensive understanding of sadistic ritual abuse. Victims of SRA come from a unique background that must be thoroughly studied and understood before a therapist can attempt to treat someone with this issue. The client must be in well-informed hands if he is going to make sense of his experiences. Their unreal experiences of growing up in a "normal" family are not normal, but are abnormal.

Lastly, a familiarity with the signs and symptoms of SRA is essential. There is some valuable information regarding satanic ritualistic signs, symbols, and important dates located in the Appendix section of this book. Although many of them often present themselves in various forms of mental illness, several of these symptoms are unique to satanic ritual abuse.

1. Lack of childhood memories. When called upon to remember a certain age, SRA victims will often find those memories are severely blocked due to the trauma associated with them. In my experience, SRA victims cannot verbalize a coherent timeline of their childhood.
2. Insomnia. Sleep deprivation is common. Since many rituals take place during the night, the children are awakened from a sound sleep and brought to the place of the ritual in a profoundly frightened state. This can lead to sleep disorders in later years. Who can sleep when all they have to look forward to is nightmares?
3. Nightmares. Survivors often relive their childhood memories through their dreams, with no memory of the abuse upon waking.
4. Physical health problems. SRA victims often suffer from physical problems in adulthood that are directly related to the physical abuse they suffered as children. For example, a child who is repeatedly hung by the arms from a rafter for any length of time is likely to suffer joint or muscle damage in later years. Also, a female child who was repeatedly raped may well experience irreparable damage to the reproductive organs.
5. Reports of bizarre behaviors by family members. Oftentimes, clients will report that family members display strange behavior, such as bringing strangers into the family unit and treating them like a family member. (Father talking on the telephone and doodling pentagrams.)
6. Frequent hand washing or bathing or checking for blood or germs. SRA victims often have repressed memories of blood on their hands

or bodies related to the rituals they endured. (Body memories: the feeling of blood on hands when none is present.)

7. Memories of rapes. The client feels as if she has been raped with no evidence to substantiate it.
8. Memories of miscarriages or childbirth without physical proof. The client feels as if she miscarried a baby or had a live birth, but there is no physical proof to substantiate it.
9. Dislike or fear of being touched. SRA victims often develop an aversion to being touched because of the abuse they have suffered.
10. Intolerance to certain sounds (triggers). Sounds can elicit memories of the former abuse, and the client develops unexplained aversion to specific sounds, i.e. a blender going in the kitchen.
11. Intolerable bright lights or strobes elicit memories of abuse. Light is often used as a form of torture in SRA abuse.
12. Sexual dysfunction. This type of dysfunction can be physical or psychological, or a combination of both. The body and the psyche are terribly abused in SRA, and often these wounds take root in sexual addiction.
13. Substance abuse. Alcohol and/or drug abuse are common in survivors as a method of escape from the memories of abuse.
14. Unexplained scars or marks on body. Many SRA rituals include cutting or burning various areas of the child's body. Once the memories of the abuse are buried, the adult survivor can no longer remember where the scars came from.
15. Being accident prone. When a client is dissociating, the normal five senses are often blunted, and the client can be unaware of his or her surroundings and possible danger or injury.
16. Unexplained dislike or fear of family members. Although an SRA victim may not consciously remember the abuse at the hands of a family member, the body remembers the harm done to it and reacts with fear or dislike at the sight of the family member that abused them. Survivors are left with strong feelings of fear or dislike - that conscious memory or explanation of "why?"

17. Fear of dogs or farm animals. SRA victims are often forced to have sex with animals. Additionally they are forced to witness the sacrifice of such animals.
18. Excessive phobias. An SRA victim can experience many fears that result in terms of adult terrors or unexplained fears that he or she cannot explain unless or until the actual memories resurface. For example, a victim might have a great fear of water which she does not understand until she remembers being repeatedly "dunked" as a child.
19. Eating disorders. These are common in SRA victims because starvation is used as a coercion method. The children are starved and then promised food if they perform horrific acts on other children as ordered by their perpetrator. The resulting affliction can range from anorexia to obesity, depending on how the starvation method has imprinted upon the child.

CHAPTER 4

Client Perspective

*However, we possess this precious treasure (The divine Light of
the Gospel) in (frail, human) vessels of earth, that the grandeur
and exceeding greatness of the power may be shown to be from God
and not from ourselves.*

- II Corinthians 4:7

IN CULT-INVOLVED FAMILIES, CASE HISTORIES will show that the majority of children ages birth to five years old experience horrific torture, controlled manipulation of incest, murder, mutilation and coercion to 'lure' other children into danger. This is their everyday existence.

When children are born and grow up in a normal home environment, there is a sense of belonging. You know that if you are learning and make a mistake, a parent will take the time to teach you and you then learn from your mistakes. There is no shaming, nor the sense that you, yourself, are a mistake.

Because of the purposeful confusion, control, and chronic chaos in an SRA environment, each child feels disengaged. You cannot be bonded with someone who is dissociative, drugged, or missing in action. Early memories of trying to have a caring adult sit and talk with you are non-existent. When children yearn to attach to caregivers, the caregivers are incapable of developing cohesive bonds. The only attachment types possible in an SRA environment are ambivalent, avoidant, or disorganized.

Deep within an SRA victim, there is the belief that she is unworthy of love. Because she is intelligent and intuitive, she will instinctively know that the only person she can trust is herself and even that trust is shaken because of constant second-guessing. This is where the chronic confusion and doubt appear. If you are four years old and you are being exposed to babies being dissected on basement altars, or your tiny hand is wrapped about a large kitchen knife and you are made to plunge it into a 'baby' and told if you ever tell, the same thing will happen to your baby sister or your pet rabbit, you believe your perpetrators. Did that really happen? Can you trust yourself to believe your own memory?

When horrific events such as this happen to you on a regular basis, you begin to feel abandonment, terror, grief and despair at the cellular level. Your only option then is to "split," or develop an alternate personality, in order to have a safe friend or place to go to.

The avoidant attachment is actually healthy for the child because of the untrustworthiness and unreliability of those around you. In SRA circles, everyone in a child's life continues to perpetuate that terror: babysitters, the cleaning people, school teachers, neighbors and your family's friends. Early on you learn that no one is safe. You can rely only on yourself. Then the terrified child becomes angry, belligerent, and starts to fight back because of the secretive injustice that is taking place. Again, a split – the child is appeased by another part of her personality, the one who is always sucking her thumb and hiding behind her mother when she is afraid. As the child continues to be exposed to the evil around her, the part of her personality that is complicit and compliant takes over and allows her to be part of the ritual ceremonies.

Another part emerges and is hounded by voices that tell the child how awful she is for participating. The child starts to understand just how bad she really is. How incapable she is of having someone listen to her or to help her. She begins to believe that she deserves the awful physical and sexual abuse she has endured because they are her fault and she deserves this punishment. Another part assumes the role of keeping everything quiet and secret.

Each distinct 'part' will take on a persona to fulfill a role. A part could be a tough guy adapting to the harsh victimization and cannot speak up/out or fight back with the perpetrator. Another 'part' could take on a three-year-old child who thinks if she stays little, the perpetrators will not continue to sexually abuse her. Then that 'part' has the adult victim 'acting' that part. Another 'part' could take on the role of a tennis ball, being so confused and tangled up inside like the innards of a tennis ball. In my experience, talking to a client about their 'parts' brings more insight than the term frequently used – as an alter. That word can evoke the word in a client's mind as *altar* and the client could dissociate.

Personal Perspective

I was often afraid of my father, but I had no idea why. It was a fact of my life that I accepted without question, and I believed it was because of his personality, which could be overpowering. My father was a physician in the armed forces, a seemingly strong man who was accustomed to giving orders and having them obeyed, both at the hospital and at home. He wasn't a yeller, never raised his voice, and had a way of keeping control at all times. But the power behind SRA is often subtle in the intimidation that keeps the underlying dread and fear active. My father's power was in his look, in his body language that could produce a 'trigger' that would paralyze me with fear because I had no idea of what was coming. In the armed forces, he was loved for being adept and on top of things but underneath in his own skin, he was intimidated by more powerful people than he. Looking back on his life, I realized that he functioned out of a very low self-esteem and used addictions and quiet power to manipulate. That power is more dangerous because you never see the 'warning' signs. If someone was drunk and raging, you would get out of the way, but when someone is sitting quietly in his chair, having his after-work scotch, it kept the survivor in me more on edge. His whisper frightened me more than a bellow ever could.

Mother was acquiescent, dedicated to keeping the house in order and keeping the peace. Father ruled the roost, so to speak, and until I was in my forties, I never questioned the fact that I couldn't remember so much of my childhood with them. I just never thought about it. It was only after I had been diagnosed with clinical depression and general anxiety disorder (GAD) that memories of my own personal hell started to surface. At the same time, thousands of miles away, my sister Katy began to remember things that greatly disturbed her and yet explained so much of her life. Together we learned the truth about my father and our early lives.

My mother never expressed an opinion of her own about anything. Dad spoke for her. It wasn't until she was well into her senior years – many years after my father had died – that her own personality began to emerge. I realized that this smart, funny, talented woman had been under a spell – perhaps even medicated – her entire married life. Was that why she didn't fight for me, why she didn't keep them from hurting me?

My father – a wonderful doctor, a faithful friend, the life of the party. My father – alcohol and drug abuser, rapist and torturer, someone who kept his wife compliant and unprotesting by drugging her. How do I reconcile the two?

Over the last 20 years, my sister and I have had many memories return, sometimes in the form of flashbacks, sometimes dreams, sometimes through a song, a piece of fabric, a spoken word, or a particular food eaten. We called these our 'flashbulb moments.'

My sister, now deceased, suffered with dissociative identity disorder, or DID. Why the abuse did not affect me in the same way is unknown to me. My theory is that the abuse did not start until I was at least two or three years old, whereas my sister was introduced to satanic rituals from the day she was born. She was bound to her abusers in a way I never could be because my personality had already begun to form, whereas hers was shaped by her abusers.

Katy and I both suffered with physical problems. When I was about three years old, my father tried to teach me how to tie my shoes. Frustrated with my ineptness, he kicked the bottom of my foot. Years later, I learned that the reason I had severe backaches when I was pregnant was two-fold: my right leg was shorter than the left, caused by the kicking, and I had a prolapsed uterus. I learned from an Emergency Room doctor that the prolapsed uterus was a sign that I had been sexually abused at an early age. Katy had even more traumatic memories:

- *Being buried alive*
- *Watching an infant being sacrificed*
- *Being forced to eat animal feces*
- *Being nailed into a coffin with snakes*
- *Being raped repeatedly*
- *Giving birth, even though Katy had no children*

We both had nightmares and phobias that we could not explain. We were frightened all the time, especially in the house in South Dakota, the one with the basement. I remember seeing rituals taking place in the laundry room in the basement: there was so much blood on the floor. I recall chickens, ducks, and rabbits being killed and disemboweled around the toilet. My sister remembered seeing parts of animals in the toilet. Small wonder we had nightmares!

There are no memories of bonding with my parents – mother or father. I remember my mother as a good cook and someone who always had lunch ready for me when I came home from school, but I have no memories of ever sitting down and actually talking *to her. When it came to raising her four children, she handled it all – my father was never involved in the day-to-day problems of raising kids. So, she was there – and yet she wasn't. My mother went through the motions of raising her children, but when we needed her most – when my father used us to carry out his rituals – she wasn't there for us. Whether because of her co-dependence or because my father drugged her into compliance, my sister and I did not have the protection we so needed against my father and his attendant followers.*

These are the memories I do have:

- *Ritual abuse around an altar*
- *Men and women in robes, swaying and chanting, covered in blood*
- *An upside-down cross nailed on the wall*
- *A man and woman taking small body parts and adding them to a pot on the stove*
- *Blood on the floor*
- *Being forced to stab a baby's body on the altar*
- *Easter pets being drowned in the toilet*
- *Poking eyes out of a live kitten as a threat to obey*
- *Oral sex with my father*
- *Being told I was adopted and would be sent back to my real parents if I did not perform oral sex on an adult or told anyone about it. I actually remember asking my mother if it was true that I was adopted. Perhaps it was a hidden hope that I really did not come from these people at all*
- *Being told by our housekeeper that if I ever told anyone about the events in our house, my sister would be killed and it would be my fault.*

Flashbulb memory: I am in a large basement with high windows, up near the ceiling. There is playground equipment on the floor in the basement. There are several children here with me, ranging from four to six years old. They are all laid out on the floor. A man and a woman are yelling orders to the children. They are making the children inflict pain on each other by having the boys push sticks into the girls' vaginas. The children are screaming. Then the boys are made to lie on top of the girls and the adults whip the boys until they bleed and lose control of their bladders and bowels. Then the boys have to clean up the girls by licking them clean. If the children do not stop screaming, they are hung from a rope attached to the ceiling. One little boy who was hung up has swung too far and he dies. The adults cut him down and he hits the floor. My memory stops abruptly.

We had no safe harbor, no one to go to for protection. Where do you turn when your father, who is also your pediatrician, is your tormenter and your mother seems to be living on another plane or doesn't care? If we told anyone, or even each other, worse things would happen. So we did what we had to do to survive: we forgot, until something in our makeup indicated that it was alright to start remembering. Even to this day, however, there are black holes in my memory. I may never remember everything that happened to me. And sometimes I hope that is true.

CHAPTER 5
Illness Associated with SRA

"Nobody knows the trouble I seen, nobody knows but Jesus."

- OLD NEGRO SPIRITUAL

THE ONSLAUGHT OF TERRORISM INVOLVED in ritual abuse includes all facets of a child's life: mental, emotional, physical, and sexual. This constant battering of the child's mind, body, and soul predict that there will be lasting damage. Often it takes years for the damage to surface, but when it does, it can be devastating. Some of the effects of ritual abuse that have been reported by survivors are:

Psychological – these arise from the mental and emotional abuse that can shatter the psyche. These disorders can take many forms, from anxiety and depression to addiction to dissociative identity disorder; the most severe mental illness of those are listed here:

Anxiety Disorders
Post-Traumatic Stress Disorder (PTSD)
Personality Disorders
Conduct Disorders
Obsessive/Compulsive Disorder (OCD)
Depression
Dissociative Identity Disorder (DID)
Suicide

Substance Abuse
Process Addictions (gambling, sexual, shopping, excessive working, etc.)

<u>Physical</u> – when a young body is ravaged by rape, beatings, suffocation, and other bodily trauma, the internal damage is long-lasting and severe.
Organic Disorders
Gynecologic Disorders
Gastro-intestinal Disorders
Sexual Disorders
Dental Disorders

<u>Adult Revictimization</u> – is caused by the layers of brainwashing to which a child is exposed, over and over again, to induce acting out. An adult can be victimized repeatedly by his or her own memories. When they resurface, it is much like reliving the horrors of childhood, one terror at a time. Revictimization can also cause the victim, once grown, to become the perpetrator, largely because he or she comes to think of ritual abuse as a normal way of life, and passes it on to the next generation. The acts imprinted upon the child become so strong that it seems natural to follow them as an adult. As an example, the author, upon the birth of her first child, actually mailed the baby's umbilical cord to her father. She did not find anything bizarre about this behavior until many years later, when her own memories began to surface. Due to dissociations and attachment disorders, clients have said they made poor choices. They have made poor job selections, partner selection, choice of poor friends and poor impulses regarding alcohol, drugs, gambling, sex, etc.

<u>Dissociative Identity Disorder</u>
   Of the many illnesses mentioned above, perhaps the most disturbing of these is dissociative identity disorder (DID), formerly known as multiple personality disorder (MPD). The psyche, overwhelmed by the onslaught of torture and abuse, can no longer bear the burden alone, and needs a safe harbor. As a result, it fractures, developing alternate personalities to handle different facets of the victim's life.

Well-known cases, such as those portrayed in the movies, *The Three Faces of Eve* and *Sybil*, document extreme personality changes, complete with different names, identities, and histories for each personality. In reality, the difference is not always marked so profoundly. A victim who is confronted by a challenge he or she cannot endure or handle might undergo subtle changes, unnoticed by all but those who know the victim intimately; and even then, it might be taken as a change in attitude rather than persona. The trait that is most revealing of dissociative identity disorder is that the main personality, when it fragments, does not remember the events that took place when a fragment or alter took over. Any stressful event might spark the fragmentation, leaving the main personality to wonder where several hours in the day disappeared to, or who had taken over the body when the main personality's defenses rose.

DID is difficult to treat and most assuredly must not be approached by a therapist who is not comfortable with treating it. Unfortunately, many therapists do not even believe that DID actually exists, but those who do, and are willing to engage a client with DID, know that the road to recovery will be a long one, fraught with difficulties and setbacks. Refer to the chapter, Treatment for Ritual Abuse Survivors, for more information on proper treatment.

The following chart, created by Dr. Janina Fisher, displays the dissociative continuum:

DISSOCIATIVE CONTINUUM

"Highway Hypnosis"	Ability to be "in the Zone"	At the moment of the trauma	PTSD	Complex PTSD	DID	DDNOS
Day Dreaming	Peak Performance	Emergency responses: staying "cool, calm & collected		Acute Stress Response		Borderline Personality Disorder

©Janina Fisher, Ph.D.

Personal Perspective

It took me many, many years to understand myself. I never thought about my personality before my memories surfaced, but once they did, things seemed to make sense. I've always been compulsive and rather regimented, but never one to keep any sustained interest in one particular activity or thing. As a child, I learned to play the piano, and played well, advancing quickly and accomplishing much. Once I became accomplished, I never went near a piano again because I had no memory of how to play or even how to read music. This is how dissociation works. A skill is begun that cannot be remembered because your mind is 'escaping' or 'going to the ceiling,' to another place and time looking for comfort. As a teen in high school, I joined the ROTC (extremely unusual for a girl of my generation), but as soon as it was finished I couldn't remember the drills. I attended school reunions but didn't recognize a single face on the people I had spent my school years with, some as many as 18 years.

As a mother of growing children, I began to sell cosmetics and became the nation's top seller very quickly. Looking back, I see that I was driven, controlling, and even ruthless in accomplishing my goal of making more and more money and prestige in the company. But I stopped selling one day and never looked back. I was dissociating. It was as if another version of me was doing these things and living this life but I have no conscious memory of it.

I know now that I had become obsessive in my drive as well as compulsive in my choices. When I was diagnosed with anxiety and depression, I learned that OCD can often be part of that unfortunate package. What may have appeared to be quirks of my personality to others were actually an outcropping of my victimization as a child. I was put in the 'cult role' of cleaner-upper at the ritual site. I developed OCD as a result of that abuse. Later in life, I was an immaculate housekeeper!

For my sister, the personality changes were more overt. She was diagnosed with dissociative identity disorder and suffered for years before discovering the truth of her condition. When she went for help, the psychiatrist she engaged treated Katy for clinical depression, but was unwilling or unable to tackle the problem of multiple personalities. As a minister, Katy would begin a presentation, excuse herself to the restroom for a few minutes, and come back a seemingly different person, with voice, gestures, and posture that were completely different. Katy did have an intensive therapy experience with two therapists and a fellow minister, but it was only for a week, certainly not enough to help her to integrate her personalities. Therapy for dissociation must be ongoing and progressive. It cannot be a shot in the dark, hoping to target the affliction and knock it out of the victim's system. Katy never received the help she so desperately needed, so she was a victim throughout her life. Her first perpetrator was her own father. Then as a grown women, she became a victim of men who preyed on someone who was too naïve and trusting to defend herself from the evils of others.

We all dissociate: it's a common fact of life. Our mind wanders, and we wonder how we got from point A to point B without consciously remembering actually driving there. Who among us has not arrived home after work without being able to recall the drive? It is not unusual. But for Katy, dissociation meant that she became another person, a different fragment of who she really was. For Katy, simple survival meant that she had to become different people in order to cope with her daily life. See the chart on page 25 to explain this phenomenon.

CHAPTER 6

Dissociation and Other Disorders

Finally, brethren, whatever things are true, whatever things are noble, whatever things are just, whatever things are pure, whatever things are lovely, whatever things are of good report, If there is any virtue and if there is anything praiseworthy—meditate on these things.

- PHILIPPIANS 4:8

DISSOCIATION: THE ACT OR PROCESS of dissociating: the state of being dissociated: as the separation of whole segments of the personality (as in multiple personality disorder) or of discrete mental processes (as in the schizophrenias) from the mainstream of consciousness or of behavior with loss of integrated awareness and autonomous functioning of the separated segments or parts (Merriam Webster Dictionary online).

Dissociation has many stages. The most commonly known form is that which causes us to block out small, everyday things – the ride to work, the paragraph in a book, the voice of someone talking to us when we are busy doing something else. These small lapses occur to everyone. The mind wanders, and the next thing you know, you have arrived at your destination, or can't remember what you just read, or have someone raising their voice to get your attention. This simple type of dissociation is not something to be concerned over unless or until it increases. The more complicated types of dissociation are classified as disorders.

According to the National Alliance on Mental Illness (NAMI), dissociative disorders are so-called because they are marked by a dissociation from or interruption of a person's fundamental aspects of waking consciousness (such as one's personal identity, one's personal history, etc.). Dissociative disorders come in many forms, the most well-known of which is dissociative identity disorder (DID). All of the dissociative disorders are thought to stem from trauma experienced by the individual with this disorder. The dissociative aspect is thought to be a coping mechanism – the person literally dissociates himself from a process or experience too traumatic to integrate with his conscious self. Symptoms of these disorders, or even one or more of the disorders themselves, are also seen in a number of other mental illnesses, including post-traumatic stress disorder, panic disorder, and obsessive compulsive disorder.

Dissociative amnesia: This disorder is characterized by a blocking out of critical personal information, usually of a traumatic or stressful nature. Dissociative amnesia, unlike other types of amnesia, does not result from other medical trauma (e.g. a blow to the head). Dissociative amnesia has several subtypes:

- Localized amnesia is present in an individual who has no memory of specific events that took place, usually traumatic. The loss of memory is localized with a specific window of time. For example, a survivor of a car wreck who has no memory of the experience until two days later is experiencing localized amnesia.
- Selective amnesia happens when a person can recall only small parts of events that took place in a defined period of time. For example, an abuse victim may recall only some parts of the series of events around the abuse.
- Generalized amnesia is diagnosed when a person's amnesia encompasses his or her entire life.

- Systematized amnesia is characterized by a loss of memory for a specific category of information. A person with this disorder might, for example, be missing all memories about one specific family member.

Dissociative fugue is a rare disorder. An individual with dissociative fugue suddenly and unexpectedly takes physical leave of his or her surroundings and sets off on a journey of some kind. These journeys can last hours, or even several days or months. Individuals experiencing a dissociative fugue have traveled over thousands of miles. An individual in a fugue state is unaware of or confused about his identity and in some cases will assume a new identity (although this is an exception).

Dissociative identity disorder (DID), which has been known as multiple personality disorder, is the most well known of the dissociative disorders. An individual suffering from DID has more than one distinct identity or personality state that surfaces in the individual on a recurring basis. This disorder is also marked by differences in memory which vary with the individual's 'alters,' or other personalities.

Borderline Personality Disorder is often a byproduct of dissociation. Those afflicted with BPD have intense, unstable relationships. The borderline personality thrives in chaos, is given to extreme moods, and regards people as all good or all bad. A client may believe the therapist to be the brightest, most helpful person in their therapy session one week; the same client with the same therapist may believe during the next therapy session that the therapist is misperceiving a look, a movement, and they will drop the therapist now and that said therapist is the worst person they have ever met. There is no loss of time or memory associated with this disorder.

Post-traumatic Stress Disorder (PTSD) is the result of a person being exposed to extreme trauma of horrifying proportions. The 'fight or flight' response is greatly exaggerated because a victim cannot discern true danger from an innocent incidence. Victims have flashback episodes, reliving the original event over and over again whenever they are triggered. They lose their sense of humor, the ability to have joy in life, the ability to sleep well, to eat well, to practice self-care, to form wonderful, authentic relationships.

Depersonalization disorder is marked by a feeling of detachment or distance from one's own experience, body or self. These feelings of depersonalization are recurrent. Of the dissociative disorders, depersonalization is the one most easily identified with by the general public; one can easily relate to feeling as they are in a dream, or being 'spaced out.' Feeling out of control of one's actions and movements is something that people describe when intoxicated. An individual with depersonalization disorder has this experience so frequently and so severely that it interrupts his or her functioning and experience. A person's experience with depersonalization can be so severe that he or she believes the external world is unreal or distorted.

One or more of the foregoing disorders are usually associated with sadistic ritual abuse, but the one most often discussed is DID, as a product of the severe trauma produced by the abuse. Dissociative identity disorder, as defined by NAMI, involves a disturbance of identity in which two or more separate and distinct personality states control an individual's behavior at different times. When under the control of one identity, a person is usually unable to remember some of the events that occurred while other personalities were in control. The different identities, referred to as 'alters,' may exhibit differences in speech, mannerisms, attitude, thoughts, and gender orientation. These alters may even present differences such as left- or right-handedness, the need for glasses, or allergies.

Often a person will begin therapy not knowing or even suspecting that he or she has DID. It is the symptoms that are of concern: memory loss, anxiety, depression, flashbacks, disorientation, and/or loss of the ability to concentrate. Those with DID often lose large blocks of time with no explanation, or will find themselves in a strange place with no memory of how they got there. They may find objects in their home that they do not remember purchasing, or encounter people they do not know, but who seem to know them. These are the hallmarks of having more than one personality inhabit the body.

DID may often be mistaken for borderline personality disorder or schizophrenia because the illnesses share certain symptoms. What separates DID is the alters. They are more than "voices in my head" as with schizophrenia or a quick change of personality to cope with a given situation, as with borderline. Alters are usually long-term co-inhabitants and begin in childhood, when the abuse was occurring and the child found herself unable to cope with it. When the limbic system of the brain is under constant attack and can no longer process the constant trauma to which it is subjected, the core personality fragments, doling out different pieces of a life filled with abuse to "others" who can handle it. The movie, *Sybil*, exhibited an excellent example of these fragments that grew to become distinct personalities. For example, within Sybil lived a tiny, helpless little girl, a tough-minded young boy, a serene young woman, and a woman on the verge of panic, among many others.

The only way to be absolutely sure that one is dealing with DID, rather than any of the other dissociative disorders, is for an alter to make herself known to the therapist. At that point, the therapist must be willing and able to undertake what will surely be one of the most intense treatments of his or her practice. Successful treatment for this disorder is largely dependent on the capabilities and caring of the clinician for the client's welfare and wellbeing.

CHAPTER 7

Attachment

For I know the thoughts and plans that I have for you, says the Lord, thoughts and plans for welfare and peace and not for evil, to give you hope in your final outcome.

- JEREMIAH 29:11

ATTACHMENT THEORY, AS SET FORTH by psychologist John Bowlby, states the bond between a child and his or her primary caregivers begins at birth and lasts throughout life. The importance of a healthy attachment cannot be overstated, nor can the danger of an unhealthy one. Bowlby believed that the primary characteristics of attachment included:

Proximity Maintenance - the desire to be near the people we are attached to

Safe Haven – when faced with fear or threat, the ability to return to the attachment figure

Secure Base – the child can move away from the attachment figure to explore the world, knowing he can return

Separation Distress – the anxiety that occurs in the absence of the attachment figure Bowlby was actually describing secure attachment. A few years later, psychologist Mary Ainsworth furthered this theory with groundbreaking research of her own, and developed four patterns of attachment, including definitions for less healthy attachments:

<u>Secure Attachment</u> – a child with secure attachment has caregivers on whom he can depend and is comfortable around them. When the

caregiver leaves, the child may become upset, but knows that the caregiver will return.

<u>Ambivalent Attachment</u>- the child becomes extremely upset when the parent leaves because he is unsure that she will return. When the parent does return, the child may want to be held, and then at the same time become aggressive toward the parent. This may be due to poor availability on the part of the parent. They will search for a substitute attachment figure and may be prone to depression.

<u>Avoidant Attachment</u>- children with this attachment style show no distress when the caregiver leaves and are apt to avoid that person when they return. They show no preference between a caregiver and a complete stranger. This is usually the result of abusive or neglectful parents. These children have trust issues, will seek out and cling to possessions rather than people. They often develop addictions.

<u>Disorganized Attachment</u>- the inconsistent behavior of caregivers can cause a confusing mix of behaviors in the child, who may view the parent as both a source of comfort and a source of fear. There is no clear attachment pattern, leaving the child confused and disoriented. The child's behavior may range from depressed to angry to completely passive and non-responsive.

Because attachment has life-long effects, a child who does not form a secure attachment will be impacted negatively in later childhood, adolescence and adulthood. Early abuse, neglect and/or trauma can lead to oppositional-defiant disorder (ODD), conduct disorder (CD) or post-traumatic stress disorder (PTSD) in a growing child. This lack of security will also have an adverse effect on relationships, as the child is unable to bond with another person as a result of trust issues. The expectation of betrayal is ever-present. If a child learns through experience that he cannot rely on the people who are responsible for his care and safety, then he also learns he cannot rely on anyone else.

CHAPTER 8

Exploring the Past

The LORD your God in your midst,
The Mighty one, will save;
He will rejoice over you with gladness,
He will quiet you with His love,
He will rejoice over you with singing.

- ZEPHANIAH 3:17

LEARNING HOW FAMILY OF ORIGIN IS IMPORTANT

A genogram is similar to a family tree: it is the construction of a family's roots. However, a genogram takes the family tree one step farther, in that the emotional and mental health history of each member is recorded. For example, a person seeking answers to his unexplained bouts of depression and anxiety, might discover that his father, uncles, grandfather, and great-grandfather also displayed symptoms of depression. Thus he would discover that his condition had genetic roots, which could, in turn, be most helpful in managing his own depression.

Genograms can help us to discover not only *who* we are, but *why* we are who we are – why we behave in certain ways, make certain choices, do the things that we do. This tool enables us to see more clearly the patterns in our lives because many of our behaviors have a genetic basis. There is also a component of 'learned behavior' from our environment of our family of origin.

A genogram can also help us to understand the behaviors of our relatives and ancestors, even if they did not pass those behaviors down to us. One person who enlisted the help of a genogram in her therapeutic sessions was seeking a basis for her PTSD. She believed it came from one instance in her childhood, but soon came to understand that there was a pattern of violence in the paternal side of her family going back four generations, including her own. Witnessing violent episodes at almost every family gathering throughout her formative years left her deeply disturbed and fearful about violent people, so much so that she was experiencing post-traumatic stress. Having gathered a deeper understanding of the root of her condition, she was able to secure more targeted therapeutic methods and overcame her terror of anger and angry situations.

It is clear, then, that genograms are immeasurably helpful in rooting out the causes of our own issues and disorders. The following page is an example of a genogram that you can use for your own family of origin. I have also included my person genogram as reference.

Exploring the Past 39

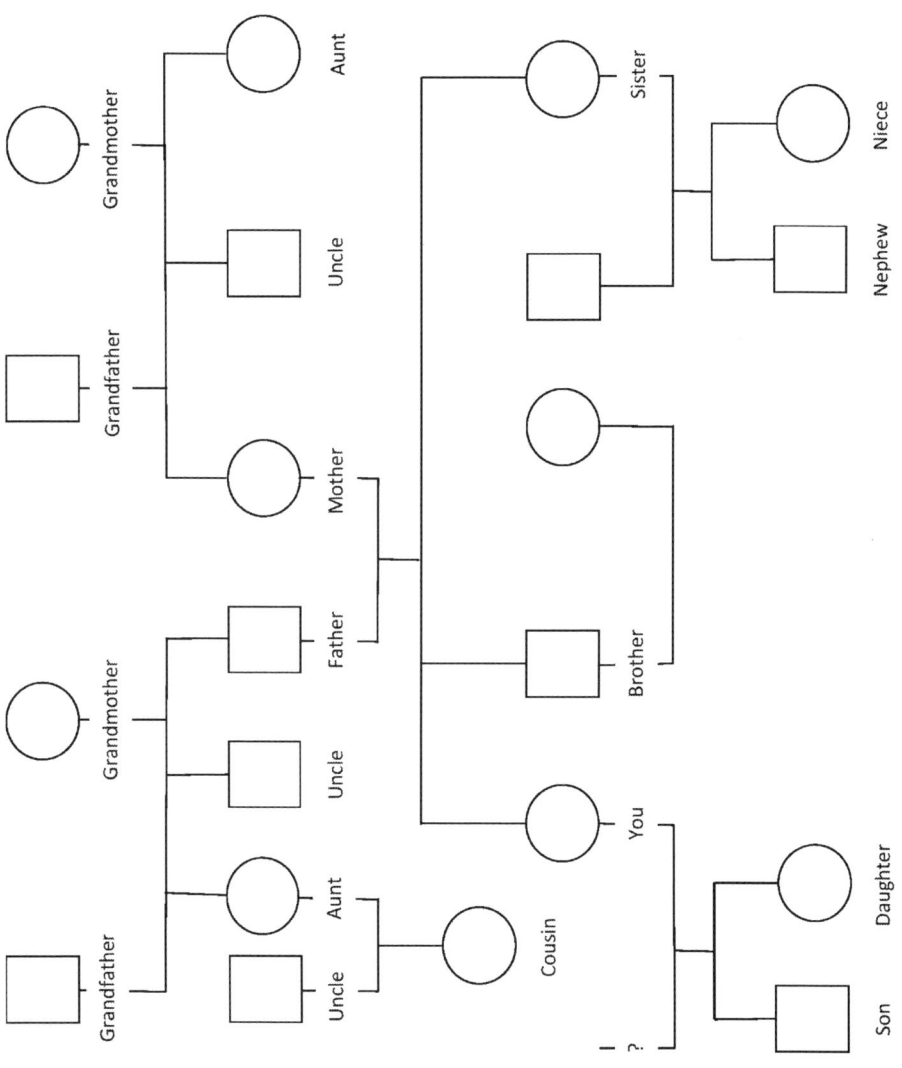

40 To Shine a Light

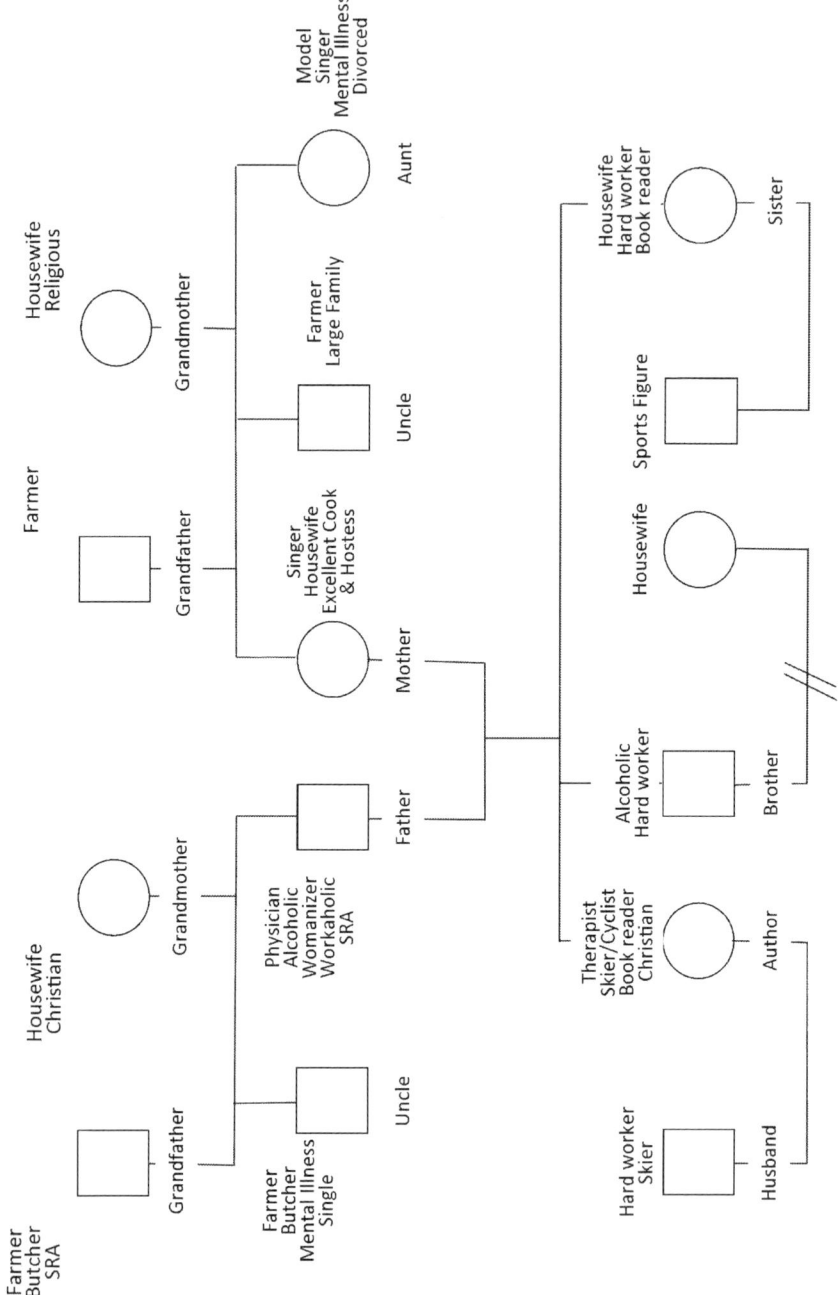

Talking to Family

Raising the subject of ritual abuse, even within the confines of family, can be tricky. Unless the memories are shared ones, it is difficult to know how much another family member knows or remembers. As with this writer, one family member shares almost all her memories, but the other siblings have no memory at all of any personal abuse. Additionally, when an SRA survivor remembers being abused by her own family, it can be almost impossible to get them to admit any wrongdoing. It can be re-traumatizing if there is no one to validate the memories. Many survivors question themselves with such thoughts as: What if I made it all up? What if I just imagined it? What if none of it is true?

To the readers who know their families will not support them in their search for truth or whose families will turn on them and call them liars, crazy, or drama kings and queens, or cut them off entirely, I say this: Do not allow yourself to fall into that trap. When memories surface, even after many years, they are your memories and they are a valid record of what happened to you.

Call a mental health clinic or a licensed therapist or licensed counselor or licensed social worker, and ask for help with someone experienced with trauma survivors. They will help you or be able to refer you to someone who has a specialty in this field.

What is important is that your family supports you in your search for the truth of your past. Even if they did not experience the same childhood horrors that you did, they can still give you unconditional love and support as you take the journey to wellness.

Personal Perspective

I was recently looking at photos of myself and my sister Katy when we were five and two and a half, respectively. We sat together on the outside steps, smiling and gazing into the camera. But although we were adorably dressed in our little pinafores and were smiling big smiles, our eyes were dead and our hands were posed in a defensive position across our laps, as if to protect our genital areas. What, I wonder, were we thinking?

Although my sister Katy and I were the only ones exposed to SRA, my other siblings did not escape unscathed. They have been damaged by our dysfunctional family. They have been beset by addictions, legal problems, boundary issues, and co-dependency. They may not have experienced the horrors that we did, but they had the same parents, the same people who were unavailable to them as caregivers or a mother and father who simply loved them for who they were.

For all their dysfunction, my other siblings do not understand the trauma of SRA. My parents, of course, deny that it ever happened. I only have Katy to rely on to validate my experiences. So there is only Katy and me. While she was still alive, we were able to lean on and console each other over the unspeakable acts we endured. We helped each other through various stages of our individual recoveries. We helped each other through the nightmares.

As much as I treasured Katy's help, I needed people closer to home on whom I could depend when the memories would get too painful to endure alone. I have been blessed with a circle of friends who offer unconditional love and support through all my trials.

CHAPTER 9
Treatment for Ritual Abuse Survivors

The Spirit of the Lord God is upon me.
Because the Lord has anointed me
To preach good tidings to the poor;
He has sent me to heal the brokenhearted,
To proclaim liberty to the captives,
And the opening of the prison to those who are bound.

✱ - Ecclesiastes 3: 1 – 8

A WELL-TRAINED THERAPIST IS VERY empathetic, a good listener, non-judgmental, has sound boundaries, and is willing to lead therapy in a measured way – not to overwhelm, not to stagnate, but to pace. He or she will be willing to ask questions and learn more about SRA/DID independently. She will treat the client with the utmost respect, cherish the time spent and feel it a privilege to help an extremely traumatized person to come to health and wholeness to the best of her ability. He/she will encourage the client to be free to do the work needed and know what it is to be done. A therapist should have a strong belief system for good and for hope. This belief system counteracts the evil to which the client has been exposed.

There is no definitive way for a therapist to determine if a new client is suffering from the effects of satanic or sadistic ritual abuse. Rather, the symptoms may present themselves as anxiety, depression, PTSD, or a host of other illnesses. Further, the client himself may not be aware of the

✱ Isaiah 61:1

underlying cause of what he is experiencing. For example, a client may at first present as having borderline personality disorder which, understandably, is difficult to treat. If the same client has a history of severe trauma, it is entirely possible that this person has been a victim of SRA. During the course of treatment, the therapist should be alert for tell-tale signs of underlying abuse: changing body language or facial expressions, vocal changes, exaggerated startle response, "switching," or a sudden change in persona. A full range of symptoms is described in the previous chapter.

Once a therapist suspects that the client is a ritual abuse survivor, the client must be treated slowly, carefully, and preferably with a combination of therapies. It is recommended that the therapist prepare herself spiritually for the journey that is about to be undertaken. This will look different to each therapist: for some, prayer; for others, meditation; for still others, centering or relaxation techniques. The diagnosis will emerge over time and will develop as the ongoing nature of assessment.

Following are elements of good therapy:

Feelings and Memory Validation: to establish a trusting and safe therapeutic environment after assessing for suicide ideation.

Cognitive-Behavioral & Cognitive Restructuring: to combat the indoctrination and cognitive distortions to which the patient has been subjected.

Ego State Therapy: to identify the characteristics of ego states/alters present. Mapping (described below) is suggested for this therapy.

Family Therapy: rather than treat the family of origin, this type of therapy addresses the inner family in a client exhibiting signs of DID. If there are alters present, this therapy will identify those who have assigned themselves such roles as Protector, Rageful, Fearful, Angry, Suicidal, etc.

Reality Therapy: to keep the patient focused on the present.

Anger Management: to help the patient manage all the emotions that have been repressed.

Spontaneous Prayer: to help center both client and therapist and reinforce the positive work that has been accomplished

The following treatment methods have been found to be quite effective in treating victims of SRA:

Talking: Talking is the most important skill for a survivor of SRA to undertake; and, it is the most difficult. Years of fear, brain washing, abuse and non-validation have programmed a client to flee, freeze or dissociate.

Talking should include built in verbal and non-verbal cues that are decided upon with the therapist and client early in the sessions. These cues give the client control and will be used to stop or slow down the process to avoid flooding and feelings of being overwhelmed. There will be times to 'apply the gas' or to 'put on the brakes' depending on the level of emotions when in session.

Two skills to incorporate while talking are grounding and breathing exercises:

Grounding: Have client place their hands in their lap; place their feet firmly on the floor and be aware of their body parts, i.e., facial muscles, tight jaw, arms and legs that may feel leaden, palpitating heart, dry mouth, etc. The client may close their eyes or leave them open. Continue exercise until a sense of control is achieved.

Breathing: Have client breathe deeply from the nose for five seconds; hold for five seconds, then exhale through the mouth for five seconds; repeat this exercise two or three times.

Both grounding and breathing exercises give control to the client, bring focus and calm the nervous system when talking. The goal is to create a calm, quiet confidence and counsel with the client.

Journaling: The simple act of writing thoughts and feelings down helps to clarify them and remove the mental blocks that do not allow for knowledge and understanding of problems. An important piece is to have a timer and set it for 20 – 30 minutes of writing. This is to control flooding and feelings of being overwhelmed. The reading of the journal will be done in the therapist's office. If the content becomes overwhelming, stop and re-ground and do breathing exercises. Though controversial, some journaling is done with the non-dominant hand for memories not in the conscious realm.

Mandala- The word 'mandala,' loosely translated from Sanskrit, means sacred circle. Used in many religions and philosophies, the mandala represents the universe and our relationship to it. It can be used as a form of meditation to bring a higher consciousness of awareness. The mandala can show us our place in the world: where we have been or where we are going. Following is an example of a mandala:

MandalaColoringMeditation.com

Instructions for how to draw a mandala can be found at http://unh.edu/health-services/ohep/spiritual-wellness/mandalas-spiritual-practice. Books about mandalas can also be found at crafts stores, such as Michael's©.

Art Therapy: Drawing accesses the creative part of the brain, allowing the client to express emotions that are guarded by the rational part of the brain. Art therapists use different modalities: pen and ink, colored pencils, crayons, modeling clay, water colors and finger paints. The use of specific colors will indicate levels of trauma. The words, designs, content are important to be seen as a metaphor for trauma. Differences in location on the paper (small – large, relationship of client to a family member/friend) are important to access. If possible, contact an Art therapist to diagnose the work.

Sand Tray Therapist: This is a specialized type of therapy. It allows the client to communicate his feelings in a non-verbal way. It is a very good therapy for children who have been traumatized and told "never tell anyone" about what has happened. By using symbols (animals, hero characters, alcohol/drug/rope, witches, fences, borders, etc.) the clients tell their story. Quickly, many will see the traumatic issues with renewed clarity and void of the flooded feelings replaced by validation from self and the therapist.

Mapping: Starting with a circle/square in the middle of a page, the client names a part of them or a feeling. As they discuss the feeling associated with that circle, they will then draw another circle either connecting or separate to the original circle/square. The map starts to take on a specific pattern of their inner parts. This map takes place over several sessions – again not to flood the client. For dissociative people, this is helpful to gain control of feelings of chaos in themselves. This practice allows the brain to free associate, accessing memories and patterns that might stubbornly elude the conscious brain.

Psychodrama – often used in group therapy, psychodrama enables the client to act out a real-life situation, and helps them to understand their motives and actions. Psychodrama is actually reframing the experience, so it is very validating to receive feedback from the other participants.

Gestalt Therapy – also known as Empty Chair Therapy, this method helps to bring awareness and acceptance to a client's actions: what they are doing, and why and how they are doing it.

Play Back Therapy – this is a similar type of therapy to psychodrama, except that others perform in the role of the client while the client observes. This is a re-authoring and retelling of the story, which enables the client to see the situation more objectively.

EMDR – helps the patient to simultaneously engage both sides of the brain and become able to face the emotions of a traumatic memory rationally and logically. Therapists are specially trained in this method to be used in the office. This can be done with specific light machines or with following the therapist's finger or a tapping method.

CARESS – Created by Lisa Ferentz, this method is effective against self-harm or abuse urges:
- CA - Communicate Alternatively
  - Drawing the body part you wish to harm, and what you want to do to it.
  - Draw the emotions you are feeling
  - Externalize your feelings by writing about them.

- RE - Release Endorphins
  - Laugh
  - Dance
  - Exercise

- SS - Self-Soothe
  - Hug a child or a stuffed animal

- Take a warm bath
- Wrap yourself in a favorite blanket and rock in a rocking chair

Additional information about how to effectively use CARESS can be found in *Treating Self-Destructive Behaviors in Trauma Survivors: A Clinician's Guide*, and *Letting Go of Self-Destructive Behaviors: A Workbook of Hope and Healing*.

Equine Therapy – Using horses with a trained equine therapist enables a client to feel a sense of control, trust, bonding and joy while gaining mastery in a new venue. Being around an animal that is non-judgmental helps to restore validation.

Canine-assisted Therapy – Using dogs and cats as a non-judgmental animal enables the client to be in control and be given responsibility for caring for something else. For trauma victims, the bonding and attachment skill is severed and animals can create the emotion of feeling love and care.

Music Therapy – Listening to music that is expressive helps to relieve stress and anxiety; bringing down heart rate and feelings of strong emotions. Different types of music, rhythms, sounds and instruments do evoke emotions that may be difficult to access. It helps with the ability to express through movement when unable to verbalize the feelings. As in talking with a client, a trained music therapist will use stopping and pausing if a client becomes flooded and overwhelmed.

Adjunct therapies are important as well:

Massage Therapy – because memory is stored on a cellular level, the trauma of abuse can show up in the body's muscle tissue. These muscles are unconsciously in a continual state of "guarding" the body. When a massage therapist works deeply through these layers, often an individual may have an emotional response or release. It often takes several sessions to reach the levels of stored memory; however, when this release happens, healing can begin. Massage therapy is an excellent tool for the re-introduction of safe touch.

Chiropractic – by the same token, trauma can cause skeletal displacement. Chiropractors work with the structure and function of the spine. By adjusting the spine, they enable the body to better function, and over time stay healthier. This holistic approach of care is non-invasive; adjustments improve immune function. A person who is free of pain can enjoy a better quality of life. Chiropractors look at the whole person, believing that every aspect of a person's life contributes to their health.

Walking- science has proven that even the simple act of walking for 20 to 30 minutes a day helps to send endorphins to the brain, relieving stress and inducing calm.

Faith-based Studies- when something as devastating as SRA has touched a person's life, it is natural to turn to faith. Studying religion and developing spirituality helps to gain perspective and equip the client to deal with the perpetrators who have victimized her.

Positive, caring friends- creating a network of loving, non-judgmental friends can be a positive influence on the healing process. Just knowing that we have a friend we can go to with any problem can be a comfort, even if all that friend does is to lend an ear and have an open heart.

The Role of Forgiveness

Faith can lead to forgiveness. Although there can and should be righteous indignation during the healing process, many levels of forgiveness are also involved in that process. Clients may ask, "How can I possibly forgive someone who did this to me?" The answer is simple: unless you are willing and able to forgive your persecutors, you cannot be released from the bondage of abuse. Clients may hear "just get over it and move on." This is referred to as 'cheap grace.' True forgiveness has empathy and compassion for the victimizer. Reconciliation is a different issue and may not happen if the perpetrators are unsafe people.

Satanic ritual abuse is generational. If something horrific is done to A in his/her generation without any awareness, help, or validation, then B in the next generation will "inherit" a propensity to do the same. This is a re-enactment of the abuse and it will continue into the third and fourth generation. The bible talks about this concept that the sins of the father will be passed onto the sons to the third and fourth generation. Addiction specialists have known this for years. When raised in an environment where alcohol, drugs, sex, smoking, gambling is present – and the children are exposed to it – the children will repeat the behaviors that are modeled. They don't know how to do anything else.

The same applies to those exposed to SRA in their environments. The drugging and brain washing techniques are used to do horrific things to one another for complicity and then repetition, even if performed while the victim is in an altered state. The victims are learning to do the same things in the next generation.

If the abused is able to get the appropriate attention, therapy, medication, prayer and support from a non-toxic environment, then there is the real possibility of healing. Forgiveness is an integral part of that healing because with forgiveness comes the ability to understand the past and change the future.

Personal Reflection

As a Christian, I know that the Lord gives gifts for those that want to flow in the Holy Spirit. Among the gifts I have received are those of word of knowledge and word of wisdom. "The word of knowledge is the revealing of a fact in existence that can only be supernaturally revealed." (Sumrall 1982) "Word of wisdom is the revealing of the prophetic future under the anointing of God." (Sumrall 1982).

Before I returned to school for my degrees and certifications, before I sought help from a mental health professional, I was a lay minister in my church. I would 'know' something about someone who would come for prayer. This was not soothsaying, but, I believe, an anointed gift from God. Used appropriately it is a powerful way for people stuck in behaviors - black and white thinking, depression, anger, rage, anxiety – to receive a message directly from God through an intermediary.

When the person who came for prayer said "Yes," and gave his/her permission, I would share this with him/her. If you were in witchcraft, this would be referred to as tapping into the outer black side. As a Christian, it is a loving and empathetic way that God can quickly break through to the hurting individual, using you to be a vessel. And then often, that person would be referred to a counselor/therapist in their church.

While in His ministry, I also led support groups under the guidance of a clinical therapist. During that time, I was first starting to remember my own past, and I continually asked the Lord to give me confirmations of what was happening to me and was it true? It became a mantra – Lord, let me be open to anything I might learn. And then I let it go, and went into a room with about a dozen women who comprised the support group.

After several of the participants introduced themselves, a small, quiet woman gave me her name and told me she was a nurse at the local air force base. She went on to tell me she originally lived in the same state I had, in the same town, and at the same base. And then she told me she had worked with my father as a pediatric nurse. Coincidence? Or God speaking? To me, this was a deep level of validation.

Not long after that, I approached a writer after a book signing because in her talk, she had mentioned that she was from my home town. When we spoke, and I told her the timeframe of my years in that town, she said, "Oh my gosh, your dad delivered my children!" Again, another level of deep validation that I knew, as I knew the truth.

Over a span of approximately two years, the coincidences and peeks into my life kept happening. Then one day, I attended a prophetic conference with a friend. We were late, so we slipped into the back row in a church that held about 300 people. The pastor called up two people from different part of the sanctuary, and then he said, "Would the lady in the dark green flowered dress come up please?" I was stunned – how could he even see me back there? When I got up to the front of the church, the pastor revealed to everyone, including me, that I had been asking the Lord about my heritage. He told me that the Lord says that my family tree is as different as North America is to South America. As he continued, something very deep inside of me knew that this was true. I immediately had a picture in my mind of witches and witchcraft. The voice of the Lord delivered through this pastor was so calming and reassuring that I was weeping uncontrollably. What was going on with me? This was a prophetic message from God through a human vessel to bring truth and validation.

These were the first instances of God beginning to 'unpeel the onion' so that I would have divine confirmation that I was going to come to understand my family of origin and what all had really happened. It gave me the enduring strength to face my past and all that it meant and to see God's hand in it from the very beginning.

CHAPTER 10

Hope for the Future

To everything there is a season,
A time for every purpose under heaven:
A time to be born, and a time to die;
A time to plant, and a time to pluck what is planted;
A time to kill, and a time to heal;
A time to break down, and a time to build up;
A time to weep, and a time to laugh;
A time to mourn, and a time to dance;
A time to cast away stones, and a time to gather stones;
A time to embrace, and a time to refrain from embracing;
A time to gain, and a time to lose;
A time to keep, and a time to throw away;
A time to tear, and a time to sew;
A time to keep silence; and a time to speak;
A time to love, and a time to hate;
A time of war, and a time of peace.

- ECCLESIASTES 3: 1 – 8

IT IS DIFFICULT, IF NOT impossible, to think about the future when you are mired in the trauma of your past. The simple act of getting through the day can be a major accomplishment and it may seem as if things are never going to change, never going to get better, and you're never going to have a normal life.

It doesn't have to be that way. While the initial trauma of remembering and healing can be all-consuming, life in its fullness can and should be treasured. Healing from SRA does not have to consume the rest of your life. By arming yourself with the tools and treatments that will help you, a positive future is possible. You may never be able to put your past entirely behind you, but you can find new perspective about it and come to an understanding of how your personality was formed and what you can do about it.

Do not hesitate to seek help. Talk to your religious leader, confide in non-judgmental friends, and above all, find a therapist who will understand what you are going through. Do not allow anyone to convince you that "it's all in your head" when you know in your heart that something happened to you and it must be faced and understood. All of these steps will correct the self-doubt you have lived with in the past. Only when the truth is known can you move forward with your life.

Personal Reflection

As strange as this may sound, I feel blessed. In discovering what happened to me and my sister, I found myself. My endurance during this journey has sometimes been weakened, but my faith never has, and that has helped to see me through the most difficult of times. I believe I was called to service as a therapist to help others to deal with this horror as well as to teach other therapists how to treat with clients suffering the effects of SRA. I have had the privilege of meeting a community of wonderful women who have had the same experiences as I, and are determined to recover. I also have a magnificent circle of family and friends who offer unconditional love and support in my enduring journey to health and wellness. This support fortifies me and gives me the needed strength to find my way. Above all, my enduring faith in God, the Father; Jesus, His son and my Savior; and the Holy Spirit, my comforter and Truth makes me thankful I am alive and here to tell my story.

CHAPTER 11
Conclusion

For God so greatly loved and dearly prized the world that He (even) gave up His only begotten (Unique) Son, so that whoever believes in (trusts, clings to, relies on) Him shall not perish (come to destruction, be lost) but have eternal (everlasting) life.

- JOHN 3:16

"PSALM 139: 15, 16. MY frame was not hidden from You when I was being formed in secret (and) intricately and curiously wrought in the depths of the earth. Your eyes saw my unformed substance and in Your book all the days were written before ever they took shape, when as yet there was none of them."

Many years ago I had a conversion experience that would set the course for the rest of my life. At the time, I had neither wisdom nor knowledge of how things would come to be. Gradually, I would come out of that dark place of oppression and intimidation and into the light that would shine on the root cause of those emotions.

Throughout this book, my desire has been to bring information, clarity and treatment options for those intended for its usage: therapists, counselors, pastors, and when appropriate clients and patients.

My fervent hope is that in the telling of our story, Katy and mine, we will say - Enough - and be the last generation to be exposed to Satanic Ritual Abuse.

I would like to bring encouragement and a renewed sense that you *can* heal from the terrors AND have a wonderful fulfilled life living as it was originally intended with peace, joy and love.

APPENDIX

For God has not given us a spirit of fear, but of power and of love and of a sound mind.
- II Timothy 1:7

Satanic Ritual Calendar

DATE	CELEBRATION	USAGE	AGE/SEX
Jan 7	St. Winebald	Animal or human dismemberment	15-33 M
Jan 17	Satanic Revels	Oral, anal, vaginal	7-17 F
Feb 2	*Satanic Revels	Oral, anal, vaginal	7-17 F
Feb 25	St. Walpurgis Day	Communion of blood and dismemberment	Animal
Mar 1	St. Enoch	Drinking of bondage blood for strength & bondage to the demons	Any age
Mar 20	**Feast Day (Spring Equinox)	Oral, anal, vaginal	Any age M/F
April 21-26	Preparation for sacrifice		
April 26-May 1	*Grand Climax	Corpus de Baahl	1-25 F
June 1	**Feast Day	Oral, anal, vaginal	Any age M/F
July 1	Demon Revels	Druids sexual association with demons	Any age F
August 1	*Satanic Revels	Oral, anal, vaginal	7-17 F
Sept 7	Marriage to beast Satan	Sacrifice, dismemberment	Infant to 21 F
Sept 20	Midnight host	Dismemberment (bonds placed)	Infant to 21 F
Sept 22	**Feast Day (Fall Equinox)	Oral, anal, sexual	Any age M/F Animal or human
Oct 29-Nov 1	All Hallows Eve	Sexual climax association with demons	Any age M/F
Nov 4	Satanic Revels	Oral, anal, vaginal	7-17 F
Dec 22	**Feast Day	Oral, anal, vaginal	Any age M/F Animal or human
Dec 24	Demon Revels	High Grand Climax	Any age M/F

* signifies most important holidays
** signifies holidays of lesser significance
Birthdays are also important.

Ref: First National Conference on Cult & Ritual Abuse, Boston, MA, June 1991.

Satanic Symbols and Rituals

- Black or brown hoods/masks and cloaks worn by cult leaders
- Pentagram symbol
- Use of fire in ritual
- Upside down crucifixes
- Altars for purpose of killing animals/babies or for dismemberment
- Use of animals for sacrifices: chickens, ducks, cats, dogs, rabbits, birds
- Animals in the ceremony: goats
- Use of knives, candles, ropes, branding iron, or guns to torture, intimidate or kill animals and humans
- Use of skeletons, aborted (miscarried) babies
- Use of buried coffins, closets or "jails," cages
- Use of spiders, snakes, rats or mice in the coffins while child is buried alive underground
- Use of drugs, alcohol or chemicals with negative statements to ridicule child
- Injected with needles and bled – drugged
- Brainwashing:
  - "Bomb planted inside you that will self-destruct if you tell"
  - "No one will ever believe you if you tell"
  - "Adopted" or "orphaned" statements to increase child's anxiety
  - Threatened with bodily harm
- Descriptions of having parents, siblings or pets killed
- Use of child pornography with cult children as models and photographed
- Use of feces and urine during ceremonies
- Chanting in ritual which becomes frenetic at time of sexual orgy with animals or humans
- Participated in mock weddings to Satan
- Had blood poured on your head
- Use of black, red, orange and yellow colors

- Held underwater
- Tied upside down over a pentagram
- Hung from a pole or a hook
- Rituals take place in barns, churches, day care settings, graveyards, or person's home
- Cannibalism of human or animals to destroy evidence
- Burned with candles

Prayers for therapy sessions:

A PRAYER FOR PROTECTION

Dear heavenly Father, we humbly bow before you, You, our Glorious God. We rejoice in the joy of our salvation. We thank you for the protection of the shed blood of Jesus Christ over our self, our ministry, our family and those we are ministering to. We stand confident in our authority. by the power of the cross and the shed blood of Jesus, to bind the powers of darkness from curses, lies or wounds that may rob us from the full and abundant life. Your power, truth and love is the path to live freely in Your will. As we enter into praying for one another, we trust You to lead us by the power of Your Holy Spirit. We trust your protections from the temptations of this world, our flesh, or the devil, for You are Lord of all. You are most powerful than anything we might face in the world. Thank you for sharing with us Your Spirit's power and compassion. Please bless our enemies by leading them into repentance and conversion. Please send your holy angels to help us in our battles. Thank you for empowering us to further Your Kingdom as Your Will is done on earth, as it is in heaven, to bring glory and honor to you. Father, Son and Holy Spirit. We ask this is the name of Jesus Christ our Lord., Amen.

PRAYER TO BE SET FREE

Dear Lord Jesus, thank you for sharing with us your wonderful ministry of healing and deliverance. Thank you for the healing that we have seen and experienced, as well as those we are yet believing for. We realize the sickness and evil we encounter in this world is more than our humanity can bear. Cleanse us now from any sadness, negativity, compulsion or despair we may have picked up. If our ministry has tempted us to anger, impatience, lust, or power; cleanse us and refresh us with Your compassion, love, grace and peace.

Please send your Holy angels to minister to us. If any evil has oppressed us in any way or taken a stronghold in our hearts, we ask You, Lord Jesus Christ to do battle on our behalf to free us. Come Holy Spirit, fill us with your power, Your peace and Your joy. Strengthen us where we have felt weak. Clothe us in your Light and Righteousness. Guard and protect us, our families, our homes, our properties, our friends from all sickness, harm, accidents or evil efforts, and give us traveling mercies home now. We praise you now and forever, Father, Son and Holy Spirit. We ask all in Jesus Holy Name. Amen

RECOMMENDED READING

DISSOCIATIVE IDENTITY DISORDER (Previously called Multiple Personality Disorder)

Boat, B., and Peterson, G. (1991). *Multiple Personality Disorder Explained for Kids.* North Carolina: University of NC, Dept of Psychiatry.

Bryant, D., Kessler, J., & Shirar, L. (1992). *The Family Inside Out: Working with the Multiple.* New York: W.W. Norton.

Calof, David (1993). *Multiple Personality and Dissociation.* Center City, MN: Hazelden Educational Materials.

Cavalcade Productions, Inc.(1993), PO Box 2480, Nevada City, CA, 95959; 1–800-345-5530. (Video 24 minutes): *Significant Others.*

Chu, James (1998). *Re-building Shattered Lives: The Responsible Treatment of Complex Post-Traumatic and Dissociative Disorders.* New York, NY: Wiley and Sons.

Cloud, H. & Townsend, J. (1992). *Boundaries.* Grand Rapids, MI: Zondervan.

Cohen, B., Gill, E., W. Lynn (1991). *Multiple Personality Disorder from the Inside Out.* Lutherville, MD: Sidran.

Friesen, J. G., PhD. (1997). *Uncovering the Mystery of MPD.* San Bernadino, CA: Here's Life Publishers.

Giancarlo, T.J. (1991, February). "Multiple Personality Disorder, A Challenge to Practitioners," Families in Society: The Journal of Contemporary Human Services, 72 (2), 95–101.

Haddock, Deborah Bray, M.Ed., MA, LP (2001). *The Dissociative Identity Disorder Sourcebook.* New York, NY: McGraw-Hill Publishing.

Howell, Elizabeth F. (2005). *The Dissociative Mind.* Hillsdale, NJ: The Analytic Press.

Miller, A. (2005). *The Body Never Lies.* New York, NY: Norton Press.

Napier, Nancy J. (1990). *Recreating Your Self: Help for Adult Children of Dysfunctional Families.* New York, NY: W. W. Norton & Company.

Ross, Colin (1989). *Multiple Personality Disorder: Diagnosis, Clinical Features and Treatment.* New York, NY: Wiley and sons.
Scarry, Elaine (1985). *The Body in Pain.* New York, NY: Oxford University Press, Inc.
van der Kolk, B., Fisler, R. (1995). Dissociation and the fragmentary nature of traumatic memories. Journal of Traumatic Stress, 8:505–525.
Watkins, John G. & Watkins, Helen H. (1997). *Ego States Theory and Therapy.* New York, NY: W.W. Norton & Co.
Winter, A. (2003). *Understanding Dissociative Disorder and Addiction.* Center City, MN: Hazelden.

MEMORIES

Leman, K. & Carlson, R. (1989). *Unlocking the Secrets of Your Childhood Memories.* Nashville, TN: Thomas Nelson.
Lesourd, S. (1987). *The Compulsive Woman.* ADA, MI: Revell (A division of Baker Publishing Group).
Minirth, F. (1995). *The Power of Memories.* Nashville, TN: Thomas Nelson.
Mask, M., Mask, J., Hensley, J., & Craig, S. (1995). *Family Secrets.* Nashville, TN: Thomas Nelson.
Terr, Lenore. (1994). *Unchained Memories: True Stories of Traumatic Memories Lost and Found.* New York, NY. BasicBooks.

SATANIC RITUAL ABUSE

C.A.S.S.A. Training Project, (1991). *Satanic Ritual Abuse.* Unpublished manuscript. (Scranton, PA).
DeYoung, Mary, (June 1996). Speak of the Devil: Rhetoric in Claims Making About the Satanic Ritual Abuse Problem. *Journal of Sociology and Social Welfare*, Vol XXII, No. 2. pp. 55–74.
Dorschner, J. (Nov. 5, 1989). The Satan Syndrome. In G. Weingarten, (Exec. Ed.), *Tropic of the Miami Herald*, Miami, FLA: The Miami Herald Publishing Co., pp. 13–19.

Dorschner, J. (Nov. 5, 1989). "Speak of the Devil". In G. Weingarten, (Exec. Ed.), *Tropic of the Miami Herald*, Miami, FLA: The Miami Herald Publishing Co., pp. 16–18.

Edwards, L. M. (1990, Special Issue). "Differentiating between Ritual Assault and Sexual Abuse". In Gerry Fewster (Ed.) *Journal of Child and Youth Care* (pp.67–90). Calgary, Alberta, Canada: University of Calgari Press.

First National Conference on Satanic Cult and Ritual Abuse, (June 1991), Satanic Ritual Calendar given as a handout. Boston, MA.

Fraser, George A. (1990). Satanic Ritual Abuse: A Cause of Multiple Personality Disorder. In the *Journal of Child and Youth Care* Special Issue. Calgary: Alberta Canada: Calgary University Press, pp. 55–66.

Hoffman, Wendy, (1991). *Identifying Characteristics of Satanic Cult Survivors.* Box 1898, New York, NY 10025; 212–932-1835. Unpublished.

Hoffman, Wendy, (1991). *Satanic Cult Abuse,* Box 1898, New York, NY 10025; 212–932-1835. Unpublished.

Hudson, Pamela S. (1990). Special Issue entitled "In the Shadow of Satan"; *Journal of Child and Youth Care*, pp. 27–54. Calgary, Alberta, Canada: University of Calgary Press.

Jones, D.P. (1991). "Ritualism and Child Sexual Abuse". In R.D. Krugman, (Ed.). *Child Abuse & Neglect: The International Journal*, 15 (3), 163–170. Elmsford, NY: Pergamon Press.

Jonker, F. & Jonker-Bakker, P. (1991). "Experiences With Ritualistic Child Abuse: A Case Study from The Netherlands." In R.D. Krugman, (Ed.). *Child Abuse & Neglect: The International Journal*, 15 (3), 191–196. Elmsford, NY: Pergamon Press.

Lanning, K. V. (1991). "Ritual Abuse: A law enforcement view or perspective." In R.D. Krugman, (Ed.). *Child Abuse & Neglect: The International Journal*, 15 (3), 171–173. Elmsford, NY: Pergamon Press.

Lawrence, Kathy J., Cozolino, Louis and Foy, David (Aug 1995). Psychological Sequelae in Adult Females Reporting Childhood Ritualistic Abuse: Richard Krugman, Editor-in Chief. *Child Abuse and Neglect*, Vol 19 (8), pp. 975–984. Elmsford, NY: Pergamon Press.

Nurcombe, Barry, MD and Jurgen Unutzer, MD. (March 1991). The Ritual Abuse of Children: Clinical Features and Diagnostic Reasoning, *The Journal of American Child Adolescent Psychiatry*, Vol 30, (2). Pp. 272—276. (1988). West Covina, CA: Passport Magazine Production.

Putnam, Frank W. (1991). The Satanic Ritual Abuse Controversy. *Child Abuse & Neglect*, vol. 15, Pp 175–179. Richard Krugman, Editor-in Chief. Elmsford, NY: Pergamon Press.

Steffon, Fr. Jeffrey J. (1991). *Satanism: Is It Real?* Ann Arbor, MI: Servant Books.

Wong, Bennet and Jock McKeen (Special Issue 1990). A Case of Multiple Life-Threatening Illnesses Related to Early Ritual Abuse. In Gerry Fewster (Editor), *The Journal of Child and Youth Care*, pp. 1–26. Calgary, Alberta, Canada: Calgary University Press.

Young, W.C., Sachs, R.G., Braun, B.C., Watkins, R. (1991). Patient's Reporting Ritual Abuse in Childhood: A Clinical Syndrome. In R.D. Krugman, (Ed.). *Child Abuse & Neglect: The International Journal*, 15 (3), 181–189. Elmsford, NY: Pergamon Press.

SEXUAL ABUSE

Allender, D.B. (1990). *The Wounded Heart: Hope For Victims of Childhood Sexual Abuse.* Colorado Springs, CO: Navpress.

Courtois, Christine. (1988). *Healing the Incest Wound.* New York, NY: Norton & Co.

Foote, C. (1994). *Survivor Prayers: Talking with G-d About Childhood Sexual Abuse.* Kentucky: John Knox Press.

Herman, Judith (1992). *Trauma and Recovery.* New York, NY: Basicbooks.

Williams, M. (1991). *Healing Hidding Memories: Recovery for Adult Survivors of Childhood Abuse.* Deerfield Beach, FL: Health Communications.

SEXUAL RECOVERY

Anderson, N. (1991). *Released from Bondage.* San Bernardino, CA: Here's Life Publishers.

Carnes, Patrick (1989). *Contrary to Love.* Center City, MN: Hazelden.
Carnes, P. (1997). *Sexual Anorexia: Overcoming Sexual Self-Hatred.* Center City, MN: Hazeldon.
Hemfelt, R., Minirth, F., & Meier, P. *Love is a Choice: Recovery for Codependent Relationships.* Nashville, TN: Thomas Nelson.
Hemfelt, R. & Warren, P. (1990). *Kids Who Carry our Pain: Breaking the Cycle of Codependency for the Next Generation.* Nashville, TN: Thomas Nelson.
Mask, M., Mask, J., Hensley, J., Craig, S. (1995). *Family Secrets.* Nashville, TN: Thomas Nelson Publishers.
Springle, P. (1990). *Codependecy: Breaking Free from the Hurt and Manipulation of Dysfunctional Relationships.* Houston, TX: Rapha.

SPIRITUAL WARFARE

Confraternity of Christian Doctrine, National Conference of Catholic Bishops & the United States Catholic Conference (1991). *New American Bible*, St. Joseph Medium Size Edition. New York, NY: Catholic Book Publishing Co.
Frangipane, Francis (1991). *Discerning of Spirits.* Cedar Rapids, IA: Arrow Publications.
Frangipane, Francis (1991). *The Jezebel Spirit.* Cedar Rapids, IA: Arrow Publications
Harper, Michael (1984). *Spiritual Warfare: Recognizing & Overcoming the Work of Evil Spirits.* Ann Arbor, MI: Servant Books.
Scanlan, Michael, TOR & Ann Therese Shields, RSM (1976). *And Their Eyes Were Opened: Encountering Jesus in the Sacraments.* Ann Arbor, MI: Servant Books.
Scanlan, Michael, TOR & Randall J. Cirner (1980). *Deliverance from Evil Spirits: A Weapon for Spiritual Warfare.* Ann Arbor, MI: Servant Books.
Sullivan, Francis, S.J. (1982). *Charisms and Charismatic Renewal.* Ann Arbor, MI: Servant Books.

TRAUMA

Amen, Daniel (1998). *Change Your Brain, Change Your Life.* New York, NY: Three Rivers Press (A division of Crown Publishing Group).

Black, Claudia (1999). *Changing Course: Healing from Loss, Abandonment and Fear.* 2nd Edition 2002. Center City, MN: Hazelden.

Levine, Peter (1997). *Waking the Tiger, Healing Trauma: The Innate Capacity to Transform Overwhelming Experiences.* California: North Atlantic Books.

Meichenbaum, D. *A Clinical Handbook/Practical Therapist Manual: For Assessing and Treating Adults with PTSD.* Waterloo, Ontario. Department of Psychology Institute Press.

Miller, Alice (1990). *For Your Own Good.* Canada: Harper Collins.

Rothschild, Babette (2000). *The Body Remembers: The Psychophysiology of Trauma and Trauma Treatment.* New York, NY: W. W. Norton & co.

Siegel, Daniel (1999). *The Developing Mind: How Relationships and the Brain Interact to Shape Who We Are.* New York, NY: Guilford Press.

van der Kolk, B. (1994). The body keeps the score: memory and the evolving psychobiology of post-traumatic stress. *Harvard Review of Psychiatry.*

van der Kolk, B., Greenberg, M., Boyd, H. & Krystal, J. (1985). Inescapable shock. Neurotramitters, and addiction to trauma. Towards a psychobiology of posttraumatic stress. *Biologic Psychiatry*, 20:314–325.

van der Kolk, B. (2001). The Assessment and treatment of complex PTSD. *Traumatic Stress.* Washington, D.C. American Psychiatric Press.

REFERENCES

Becker, Kariker, Overkamp & Ratz. (2007) Extreme Abuse Survey. http://extreme-abuse-survey.net/

Bowlby, John. Theory of Affect Disorder. http://psychology.about.com/od/loveandattraction/ss/attachmentstyle.htm

Clark, Terri A. (1993). *More than One.* Nashville, TN: Oliver-Nelson Books.

Ferentz, Lisa. (2012) C.A.R.E.S.S. model.

Fisher Ph.D., Janina. (2011). Psychoeducational Aids for Working with Psychological Trauma. Tenth Edition. *Dissociative Continuum.*

Friesen Ph.D., James G. (1991). *Uncovering the Mystery of MPD.* San Bernardino, CA: Here's Life Publishers.

Haddock, Debora Bray. (2001). *The Dissociative Identity Disorder Handbook.* Chicago: McGraw-Hill.

National Alliance on Mental Illness (NAMI). (2013). Dissociative Identity Disorder. http://www.nami.org/template.cfm?template=/contentManagement/contentDisplay.cfm&contentID=23048

North American Association of Christians in Social Work (NACSW). (2011). www.nacsw.org.

Sakheim, David and S. Devine. (1992). *Out of Darkness: Exploring Satanism & Ritual Abuse.* New York: Lexington Books.

Sumrall, Lester. (1982) *The Gifts and Ministries of the Holy Spirit.* New Kensington, Pennsylvania: Whittaker House.

The Amplified Bible. (1987). Grand Rapids, Michigan: Condervan Publishing.

The Holy Bible. New King James Version.(1982). Nashville: Thomas Nelson.

Made in the USA
Charleston, SC
14 March 2015